EXETER
IN ROMAN TIMES

by

Aileen Fox MA FSA

ISBN 978-1-80413-182-4 Paperback
ISBN 978-1-80413-183-1 PDF

Published by the University of Exeter
Printed in England by James Townsend and Sons Limited, Exeter

Preface

THE University of Exeter (formerly the University College of the South West) has through its Department of History always taken a great interest in local history, and since the last war has actively encouraged archaeological research.

In 1952 my predecessor, Professor W. N. Medlicott, wrote in a preface to Aileen Fox's book, *Roman Exeter,* 'Exeter, which emerged from German bombing with two great open spaces to east and west of the Cathedral Close, took advantage of the destruction of so much of the Medieval and Georgian city to investigate its Romano-British origins.' In 1971, as a result of planned demolitions within the city, once again large areas lie open, an opportunity for the archaeologist. This booklet has been specially written by Lady Fox, Senior Lecturer in British Archaeology in the University of Exeter, and all profits from its sale go towards the cost of the present excavations. It is a valuable contribution from the recognised authority on *Isca Dumnoniorum.* Her excavations in 1945, 1946 and 1947 (when she was a more junior member of the University College), which were described and evaluated in her book, contributed a completely new chapter to the ancient history of this city; and her later digs, necessarily on a smaller scale, filled in some of the gaps. But no one was more aware than she how much remained to be done, how much material lay, despite the cellars, beneath the existing buildings. And in 1970 she took the lead in urging that the utmost should be done before the property developers took over the vacant lots. Her enthusiasm led to results. Now, as on the previous occasions, the University of Exeter and the City, with the help of the Ancient Monuments branch of the Ministry of the Environment and other interested parties, are working together to explore the city's past. The team is led by Mr John Collis, MA, an archaeologist in the Department of History and Mr Michael Griffiths, BA, on the staff of the Royal Albert Memorial Museum.

Men build up and archaeologists scrape down to disclose the various levels of occupation. All layers of deposit, including post-medieval and medieval, will be investigated. The scientific excavators of the modern age can make much of a few coins, bits of pottery, and the other débris of past generations. It is unlikely that much important material treasure will be found under Exeter; but it is certain that as a result of the present excavations and those which will follow we shall know much more about the history of our city.

FRANK BARLOW
Professor of History, University of Exeter

April 1971

EXETER IN ROMAN TIMES

EXETER in Roman times was the capital city of the South West, the administrative centre for a region covering present-day Devon, Cornwall and west Somerset. Nearly all the people who lived in the city or in its territory were of native British descent; some lived in Roman-style houses in the town or on their country estates, others in stone or wooden huts that in essentials had changed very little for a thousand years. Collectively they were known as the *Dumnonii,* meaning 'The people of this land'; *dumno* is a Celtic word meaning land or territory. Their city was called *Isca Dumnoniorum* (Isca of the Dumnonii), named after the river on which it was situated, meaning according to some philologists a river abounding in fish, an early tribute perhaps to Exe salmon. The same Celtic name, *Eisca* or *Wysc,* was given to other rivers, but survives in a slightly different form, for example the Usk in South Wales, the Axe in Devon and Somerset or the Esk in south-west Scotland.

In its final form *Isca* was a fine walled city nearly 100 acres in extent and entered by four gates. It was situated on a hill slope with the circuit of its walls (fig. 1) enclosing the summit of Rougemont (now the site of the Norman and later Castle) and descending 150 ft to the West gate in the river valley (near the present St Mary Steps church). The interior was crossed by a Roman grid of well-metalled streets, fronted by shops and houses built of stone or half-timbered. In the centre where the ground was more level, there were the public buildings, the *Forum* which was the administrative centre as well as a market and place of assembly, and the Baths, which were a favourite place of relaxation in Roman times. There would also be pagan temples in their own enclosures where both Roman and Celtic deities were worshipped, and in all probability a Christian church.

Such a city, however, did not appear full fledged; it was the product of an historical process of development and growth extending over some 400 years. It is the purpose of this booklet to try to explain how this came about.

The sources on which this account is based are archaeological, for there is very little relating to this area in classical writers except place-names, which are to be found in Ptolemy's Geography and in the road-books, the Antonine Itinerary and the Ravenna Cosmography. First there is the evidence of chance finds of objects, including many coins, which were carefully recorded in the mid-nineteenth century by a local antiquary, Captain W. T. P. Shortt; some of these have found their way into the City Museum's collections at Rougemont House. Secondly there are the structures, some like the City Wall still surviving, others including the gates, demolished in the nineteenth century: records of these were collected and summarised by the late Professor Richard Goodchild in 1954. They provide the clues to the layout of the Roman city. Thirdly and most important there are the records of scientific excavation carried out in Exeter during the last thirty years, principally after the end of the War, when large areas devastated by German bombing were available for investigation. By means of intensive study of stratigraphy, these established a chronological framework and the principal stages in the historical development of the Roman city. It was however not until the excavation of the South Gate in 1964–65 that the military character of the first Roman occupation was established.

There are of course still many gaps in our knowledge of the topography and history of *Isca*. The current excavations sponsored by the City Council and Exeter University with the support of the Ancient Monuments division of the Ministry of Environment should make a significant contribution and perhaps produce some surprises.

The known history of the Roman city falls into three structural phases:

(i) the military occupation and the native suburban settlement (*Cannabae*), about A.D. 45–75;

(ii) the open city, about A.D. 75–160;

(iii) the walled city, from the late second century onwards.

These will now be described in order.

THE MILITARY OCCUPATION

There is no evidence that Exeter was a fortified settlement of the Celtic peoples in pre-Roman times despite its obvious attraction as an end-spur site at the head of tidal water, offering a ready-made defence and access by river. The numerous hill-forts in the district are on higher ground, such as Woodbury Castle on the Common or Cotley on Haldon. There is some indication that the Dumnonian people in the area in the first century A.D. were giving way to the neighbouring tribes of the Durotriges in Dorset (fig. 2), for their characteristic black pottery ribbed bowls and coins have been found in east Devon and also appear in the earliest Roman levels in Exeter. The Durotriges strongly resisted the Roman conquest as is evident from the attacks on their great *oppida* at Maiden Castle and Hod Hill in Dorset. It was therefore to be expected that the campaign undertaken in A.D. 44 by Vespasian, a future Emperor, in command of the Second Augustan legion and its associated auxiliary troops, should be pushed to its logical conclusion and be carried westward to the Exe.

Once the battles were over, it was necessary for the troops to garrison the newly conquered land and to police the native inhabitants. Accordingly forts were built in strategic positions in which small mixed detachments or whole units were stationed. The forts were rectangular, defended by a turf rampart and ditch, with timber gates and towers. The soldiers were housed in timber barracks; there were buildings of similar construction for the administration (the *principia*), for the commandant (the *praetorium*) as well as granaries (*horrea*) and stores. The layout of a fort of this period is manifest at Hod Hill, where a mixed detachment of legionaries and auxiliaries was quartered in a corner of the Durotrigian hill-fort. At Exeter a short length of the defences of such a fort have been found, in South Street in 1964. These consisted of a V-shaped ditch eight feet wide, cleanly cut four feet deep into the natural gravel, and the base of a timber-faced rampart running roughly north to south, below and at right angles to the later city wall (plate I). Wedged in the ditch bottom there was the neck of a 'Rhodian' amphora with peaked handles, a characteristic import of the mid-first century. From the situation it would appear that the defences belonged to the north-west angle of a fort from some four to seven acres in extent, situated on relatively level ground south of the later city and tactically well placed to command the river crossing (fig. 1). To the north and south the probable outline of the fort is defined by the fall to Coombe Street and to the Shutebrook valley in Holloway Street.

The site however was low-lying relative to the relief and needed to be supplemented by a look-out post. On the crest of Stoke Hill five hundred feet up and $1\frac{1}{2}$ miles north-east of the city, air-

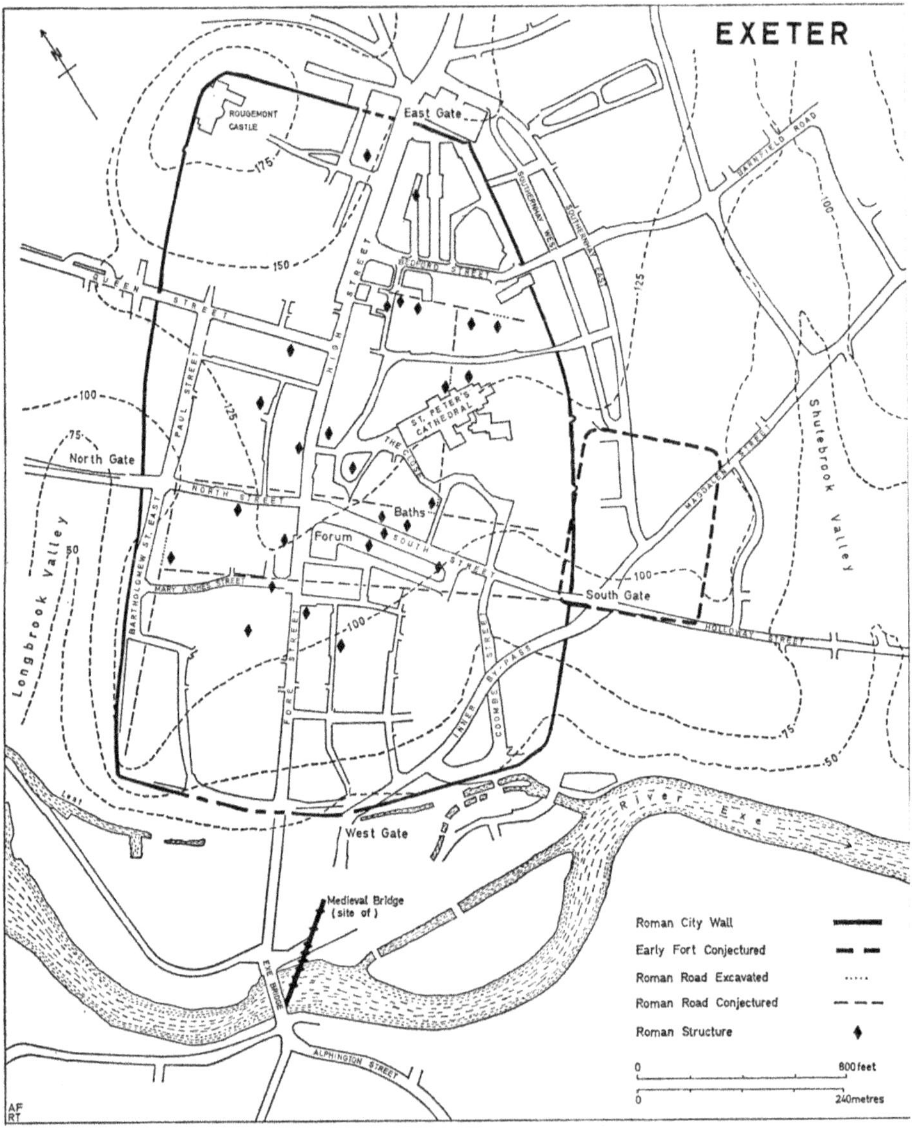

EXETER

ROUGEMONT CASTLE

East Gate

North Gate

ST. PETER'S CATHEDRAL

Baths

Forum

South Gate

West Gate

Medieval Bridge
(site of)

River Exe

Longbrook Valley

Shutebrook Valley

Roman City Wall	▬▬▬
Early Fort Conjectured	▬ ▬
Roman Road Excavated	.....
Roman Road Conjectured	‑ ‑ ‑
Roman Structure	◆

0 ——————— 800 feet

0 ——————— 240 metres

Fig. 1 Plan of the Roman city and conjectural outline of the early fort.

photography revealed the plan of a fortlet, a double squarish enclosure, very similar to others of this period on the north Devon coast at Old Burrow and Martinhoe. Excavation in 1956 at Stoke Hill revealed no trace of a wooden signal tower in the inner enclosure, but the site itself commands a wide panoramic view over the Exe, Creedy and Clyst valleys, as well as to the coast. The Exeter fort and associated Stoke Hill fortlet were part of the early Roman frontier system and were linked by well engineered roads such as the Fossway with others in the territory of the Durotriges in Somerset or of the Dobunni in the Cotswolds (fig. 2).

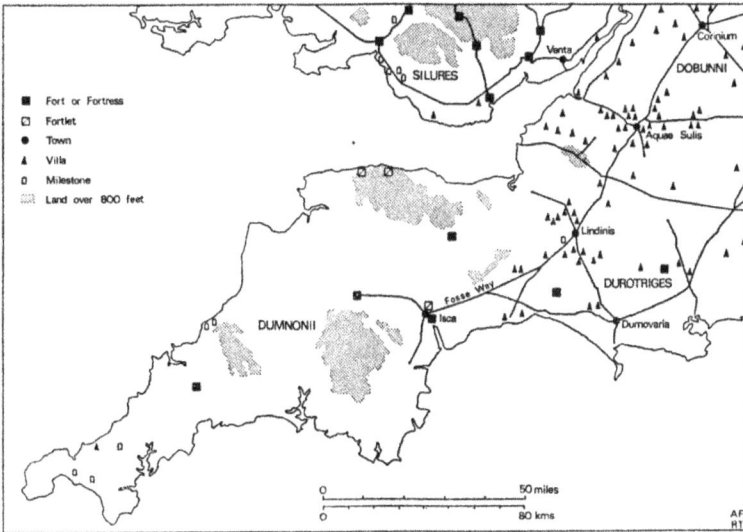

Fig. 2   The South West in Roman times (based on the Ordnance Survey map of Roman Britain, with additions).

It is uncertain how long the Exeter fort was in use or whether it was replaced by another on the larger later city site. During the reign of Nero (A.D. 54–68) the Roman army again took the offensive against the Dumnonii and advancing into mid-Cornwall established a fort at Nanstallon on the Camel west of Bodmin, as well as maintaining its hold on the north Devon coast. It is therefore likely that Exeter was still under military control until the end of the reign.

In the meantime a native settlement had developed in the area north of the fort and to the west of the present South Street. Remains of timber buildings were found here in 1946 on either side of a narrow metalled roadway with a central drain leading downhill towards the river. The rectangular houses were constructed with a framework of driven posts with an infilling of bedded wattle-work. Inevitably as in any city excavation their remains were incomplete, but one had a principal room 37 x 25 ft with a central hearth built of red tiles, flanked by other rooms and a verandah (fig. 3). The adjoining room had been

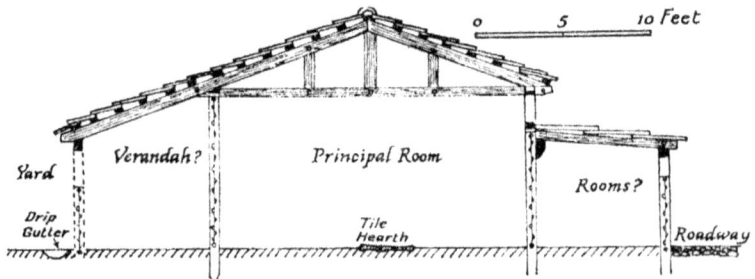

Fig. 3   Reconstructed section of an early Roman timber house, South Street 1946.

used both as a kitchen and a workshop; the clay floor was covered with dirt, animal bones, soot and charcoal; and there were also pieces of crucibles used for heating lead or enamel testifying to a small local industry. Other remains of early metal working were found in 1959 in Bartholomew Street East, where there were furnace holes and smelting hearths as well as the clay nozzles from the bellows (*tuyères*), crucibles and iron slag. Here too there was a well-metalled east to west road 14 ft wide, flanked by timber shops or houses, two rooms deep. These had been destroyed by a fierce fire about A.D. 80–85 which had burnt the daub walls to a brick-like consistency. The occupation in South Street had ended some five to ten years earlier.

Whilst the first settlement probably began as an adjunct to the military post, as a place where craftsmen and traders could find a ready market for their wares and where the soldiers could satisfy their domestic needs when off-duty, it is clear that during the thirty years after the conquest a prosperous township in embryo developed at Exeter. Coins of the Emperors Claudius, Nero and Vespasian circulated

Plate I   South Gate excavations 1965. Ditch of early fort with amphora neck at bottom.
The late second century clay rampart overlies the ditch.   *Photo A. Fox.*

Plate II   Bear
Street excavations
1953. Stone conduit
with tiled floor
carrying waste
water from the
Public Baths.
Photo A. Fox.

Plate III The city wall west of the Inner By-Pass. The Roman core and facing stones are visible on right. *Photo Exeter University.*

Plate IV The city wall in Southernhay. Twenty courses of Roman masonry can be seen above the chamfered plinth. *Photo Exeter University.*

Plate V   South Gate excavations 1964. Remains of the Roman gate tower: in foreground the early fort ditch.   *Photo A. Fox.*

Plate VI   The South Gate in the early nineteenth century, showing the round arch on the inner side.   *Photo Exeter City Library.*

Plate VII   Roman glasses found on site of British Home Stores, Fore Street, 1952.

Photo Exeter University

Plate VIII   South Street excavations 1946. Sherd of cooking pot with an incised Christian symbol, the Chi-Rho. *Photo Exeter University.*

rooms, (*tepidarium* and *caldarium*) and then returning to the *frigidarium* for a final cold plunge.

New roads were also constructed in the city at this time and others repaired. They were made with a foundation of stiff clay and stones or cobbles, and surfaced with fine river gravel, with a camber to throw off rain water. It was customary for the Roman surveyor to fix the lines of the main streets at right angles to each other, thus dividing the town into blocks (*insulae*) of a chequer-board pattern. In Exeter, however, the up-and-down character of the site may have prevented this in certain parts of the town and some irregularities are already apparent in the plan (fig. 1). It is also clear that the medieval streets in general do not conform to the Roman line; for example Catherine Street and South Street overlie remains of Roman buildings. The line of one major road directed to the port settlement at Topsham was established in 1964 at the South Gate and another to the east of the Baths in Bear Street which may have been originally the military road to the north, but the principal east to west thoroughfare, connecting with the Fossway and leading to the river crossing, has so far eluded detection. The river with its small islands was probably crossed by a series of wooden bridges, with stone piers in the main stream. Roads on the west bank of the Exe are known to continue south-west across Haldon and north-west to North Tawton and Cornwall (fig. 2). It must be pointed out that the road lines in the town conjectured on fig. 1 are based on short and incomplete sections of metalling and are liable to be corrected by further discoveries.

The extent of the city in the late first and second centuries probably differed little from the walled city of the third century which succeeded it. Waste from a tilery found in Post Office Street in 1947 and from metal workers' furnaces near the South Gate in 1965 were likely to be on the perimeter. Shops and houses were probably mostly still half-timber buildings, but with stone foundations and concrete floors. There is no indication that the prosperity noted in the first century (page 10) continued for long after the great effort of monumental building in the 80s. Coins of the second century decline proportionately in comparison with those of the first century. This in turn must reflect the failure of Roman civilization among the Dumnonii in Devon and Cornwall. Due to the predominantly highland character of much of the peninsula and the lack of communications, romanisation appears to have been ineffective. No town and only one small villa—a house built at Magor, near Camborne in the Roman style—is known west of freely, fine red Samian ware was plentiful and glass and fine pottery was also imported from Gaul and Germany. The two greenish-blue glass vessels (plate VII) found in a rubbish pit on the site of the British Home Stores in Fore Street in 1952 typify the high quality of imported goods available in *Isca* at the end of the first phase of the city's development.

THE OPEN CITY

By A.D. 75–80 all troops had been withdrawn from the South West for they were needed to garrison Wales and for Agricola's campaigns in Scotland. The Dumnonii had been pacified and were now to be recognized as a *Civitas,* a tribal group of citizens governing themselves in the Roman manner, subject to the provincial Governor and to the financial demands of the imperial Procurator in London. There would be a Cantonal Council (*Ordo*) of a hundred decurions elected from the Dumnonian land-owners and merchants, two of whom acted as magistrates each year whilst two others (*aediles*) took charge of the public services. Consequently their city centre needed to be laid out afresh, with public buildings of stone replacing the small timber constructions. An extensive gravelled courtyard with surrounding colonade which was laid down on top of the road and demolished South Street houses, may well be part of the administrative centre, the *Forum*. The buildings would comprise a great hall, the *basilica*, the *curia* where the Cantonal Council met, a row of offices for the aediles and magistrates, and a market of small shops, all arranged around an open courtyard, the Forum proper, where citizens could assemble. Close by were the Public Baths (*Thermae*), of which the large cold plunge bath 52 ft long and 4 ft deep was uncovered in the Deanery garden in 1934, and the conduit carrying off the waste water which was found in Bear Street in 1953 (plate II). Owing to the slope southwards to the combe, the building was supported by massive concrete foundations which were exposed when South Street was widened in 1951. When completed, the building would have contained a set of rooms heated by hot air from a furnace, which circulated round small pillars (a hypocaust) below the thick concrete floors, and in flue tiles in the walls: tanks of hot water produced a steamy atmosphere as in a Turkish bath. There might also be a room with dry heat (*laconicum*) from a separate furnace, inducing a quick sweat as in the Scandinavian Sauna bath. Undressing rooms were provided (*apodyteria*) and an open court (*palestra*) where physical exercises could be performed before entering the heated the Exe (fig. 2). The native population continued to live in settlements like Chysauster, near Penzance, with little change in their mode of life or improvement in their economy. Consequently the tax yield would be small and uncertain and opportunities for trade were limited.

THE CITY DEFENCES

In the latter part of the second century it would appear that the *civitates,* the tribal self-governing organizations in Britain, were instructed by an imperial edict to fortify their cantonal capitals. Hitherto, with a few exceptions like Silchester, they had been un-defended. At Exeter, as elsewhere, the perimeter was first defended by a rampart and ditch, later to be replaced by a stone wall. The rampart, which still survives as a massive bank in the Bishop's Palace garden, consisted of layers of clean clay and gravel dug from the external ditch; originally it was about seven or eight ft high and 25 ft wide. Judging by the archaeological material found underneath it, principally some decorated Samian bowls near the South Gate (fig. 4), the rampart was constructed some time after A.D. 160, possibly in the time of Albinus the governor of Britain who made an abortive effort to become Emperor between A.D. 193–7.

There were four gates presumably in the same places as the imposing medieval and Tudor structures which were unfortunately removed because they obstructed traffic in the early nineteenth century. During excavations at the South Gate in 1964 no sign of emplacements for a Roman timber gate were found and it was concluded that the remains of the stone gate were probably contemporary with the ramparts, as at the neighbouring cantonal town of Cirencester. There was a difference in the foundations and the masonry was not bonded into the later wall, which was butted up against the gate tower. Very little remained of the gate (plate V), only the bottom courses of the 16 ft square tower on the west side of the entrance, which was probably through a central arch-way twelve to thirteen feet wide, flanked by separate footways. It is pos-sible that the round arch that is shown on the inside of the South Gate in early nineteenth century prints was a Roman survival (plate VI).

After an interval in which brushwood and vegetation had grown on the rampart in places, *Isca* was refortified. The front of the rampart was cut back, a trench was dug for a loose foundation of the local Volcanic stone, Exeter Trap, quarried on Rougemont; on this a massive wall ten to eleven ft thick was built (plate III). The external facing consisted of square cut blocks of Trap, regularly coursed but not uniform in size,

13

Fig. 4   Decorated Samian bowls, of mid-second century date found beneath
the rampart at the South Gate 1964. *Drawn by K. Atkinson.*

with a chamfered plinth at ground level (plate IV). The core of the wall
was of rubble, often pitched herring-bone fashion and set in coarse
yellow mortar. The rear face was left rough where it backed up against
the rampart; above that, the wall was narrowed, being set back
internally and faced with small blocks up to the level of the wall-walk,
about twenty feet high above the plinth. The exact date of construction
is not known but it was certainly during the third century, and probably in the reign of Severus or his sons, A.D. 197 to 235.

It is possible to follow the two-mile long course of the wall in
Exeter and in so doing to appreciate the massive effort and the skill of
the Dumnonian masons and how advantage was taken of the defensive
qualities of an end-spur site. On the north the wall was aligned on the

crest of the steep slope to the Longbrook valley (fig. 1) but dipped to a shallow re-entrant where the North Gate was situated. Continuing north-east, it rose again and encircled the volcanic knob of Rougemont (now the Castle in Northernhay Gardens) and then descended to cross the spur on which the East Gate was sited on the line of High Street. The defences then bore away south-westwards, following (in Southernhay) a course parallel to the Shutebrook valley and dominating its western slope. As far as the South Gate, the descent was gradual but thence to the river it was steep, enclosing the small combe (plate III). Beyond the south-western angle, the wall and rampart were situated just above the flood plain; the river, then tidal, and its islands provided both a means of access to the city and a line of defence.

Although the line of the wall is clear, the Roman masonry has been extensively altered in medieval times, using a variety of stones quarried from Pocombe, Heavitree and Beer. Much of the wall was refaced, and the foundation underpinned where the external ground level was lowered; buttresses were also added on the eastern side (Southernhay) to cover with flanking fire the line of easy approach. The Roman work however can always be distinguished by the chamfered plinth and courses of purplish vesicular Trap blocks.

EXETER IN THE THIRD AND FOURTH CENTURIES

After the completion of the defences, *Isca* and the canton seem to have entered on a period of relative prosperity, which lasted through the third and first half of the fourth centuries. The province of Britain escaped the barbarian invasions and the military anarchy of the third century, though subject to Saxon raiders and to the economic troubles and consequent inflation. In Dumnonian territory milestones show that roads were made or repaired under the Emperors Gordian III (A.D. 238–240) and Postumus (A.D. 258–268) probably reflecting new activity in tin production. Pewter vessels with a high tin content are also indicative of a new industry in the area. A number of coin hoards show that money was circulating more freely among the Dumnonii even if it was in the debased and inflated currency of the Gallic emperors which was later repudiated. The threat of Saxon raiders may have caused the look-out post on Stoke Hill (page 9) to be manned again in the time of the Emperor Carausius, A.D. 287–293.

In the city itself there were alterations to the Baths in the first half of the third century, and the only dated mosaic, a guilloche pattern in three colours, from a house in Catherine Street has also been assigned to this period. In all, remains of ten tesellated pavements have been recorded in Exeter, from the eighteenth century onwards; one in Waterbeer Street consisted of intersecting arcs of coarse white tesserae on a red ground. Houses were now stone-built, with mortared walls of Trap, and cement floors, occasionally with under-floor heating by hypocausts; no complete house plan has yet been recovered. A possible temple was recorded in Broadgate; nearby four bronze statuettes were found in 1832, representing Apollo, Mars, Mercury with his cock and a goddess with a cornucopia, perhaps Ceres or Fortune. No inscriptions have been found or figure sculpture, due to the lack of suitable freestone in the locality and perhaps to the lack of demand. Exeter's participation in overseas trade is indicated by discoveries of Greek issues of Roman imperial coins, mostly Alexandrian of third century date.

It is unfortunate that there is so little detailed knowledge about the later history of Exeter; the upper Roman strata containing remains of the fourth century have nearly always been removed by subsequent builders. The coin list with over three hundred coins listed for the first half of the fourth century, compared with two hundred for the whole of the third century, indicates a period of new prosperity in the city. This is in keeping with a general revival in the province as a whole under Constantine (A.D. 306–337) consequent on Diocletian's reforms of the military and administrative systems throughout the Empire. Christianity was now an official state religion and in Exeter the existence of a Christian community of a humble kind is known from a Chi Rho or Chrism sign pecked on a black cooking pot (plate VIII); this is a monogram of the first two Greek letters of the name of Christ. The pot was probably used to take offerings of food and drink to a church or Christian meeting place.

In the second half of the fourth century, particularly after the concerted barbarian attacks of A.D. 367, Romano-British civilization began to go finally downhill. In Exeter the Forum was abandoned about A.D. 380 and a 9 in. layer of dark humic soil accumulated over the surface. Two shallow pits were cut through it and used for burying rubbish, chiefly food bones, showing the decay in corporate town life. There were fewer coins in circulation and hardly any of the Theodosian series of A.D. 388–402, the last to be issued from the Gallic mints; indeed the coins end effectively with those of Gratian in A.D. 383. Doubtless people went on living in the walled city but the upkeep of public buildings was beyond them and for how long the administration of the canton was effective is uncertain. A lady buried near Split (Jugoslavia) in A.D. 425 is described on her tombstone as a Dumnonian citizen by birth (*Civis Dumnonia*) so the canton survived in name. Gildas, writing in the sixth century also refers to the rulers of Dumnonia, but in unflattering terms. The distribution of the memorial stones of Celtic rulers and of imported Mediterranean pottery suggest that the centre of power had shifted away from *Isca* in the post-Roman epoch. The Saxons therefore had little difficulty in taking over the city and founding the monastic church dedicated to St Peter in the mid-seventh century.

Bibliography

Those interested in obtaining further information about the sites and subjects mentioned in the sections of this booklet should consult the publications listed below.

Finds before 1942

R. Goodchild in Aileen Fox, *Roman Exeter*, 1952, p. 98.
W. T. P. Shortt, *Sylva Antiqua Iscana*, 1840.
W. T. P. Shortt, *Collectanea Curiosa Antiqua Dumnonia*, 1841.

The Military Occupation

South Gate fort: A. Fox, *Proc. Devon Arch. Soc.,* 26 (1968), p. 1.
Stoke Hill signal station: A. Fox and W. Ravenhill, *Trans. Devonshire Assn.* 91 (1959), p. 71.

The Cannabae

A. Fox, 'Roman Exeter, origins and early development,' in *Civitas Capitals of Roman Britain*, ed. J. Wacher, 1966, p. 46.
South Street: A. Fox, *Roman Exeter,* 1952, p. 7.
Bartholomew Street East: A. Fox, *J. Roman Studies.* (1960), p. 231.
Glass: A. Fox and D. B. Harden, *Proc. Devon Arch. Soc.* IV (1951), p. 106

The Open City

Forum: A. Fox, *Roman Exeter,* 1952, p. 17.
Baths: M. Neilson, *Proc. Devon Arch. Soc.* II (1934), p. 72, and A. Fox, *Roman Exeter,* p. 18.
Conduit: A. Fox, *Proc. Dev. Arch. Soc.* V (1953), p. 30.
Roads: A. Fox, *Proc. Dev. Arch. Soc.* 26 (1968), p. 6.
The Site: W. Ravenhill in *Exeter and its Region*, British Association Handbook, 1969, pp. 123-8.

The Defences

A. Fox, *Roman Exeter,* pp. 19 and 57.
The South Gate: A. Fox, *Proc. Dev. Arch. Soc.* 26 (1968), p. 9.

Third and Fourth Centuries

Mosaics: Catherine Street, A. Fox, *Roman Exeter,* p. 21.
Waterbeer Street, A. Fox, *Roman Exeter,* p. 99.
Statuettes: J. Milles, *Archaeologia,* VI, 1782, p. 1.
Chi-Rho: A. Fox, *Roman Exeter,* p. 92.
Coins, R. Goodchild, in *Roman Exeter,* p. 104.
S. Pearce, *Trans. Devonshire Assn.* 102 (1970), p. 19.
R. Goodchild and J. G. Milne, 'Greek Coins from Exeter',
Numismatics Chronicle, XVII, 1937, p. 124.

The Canton

A. Fox, *South West England,* 1964, ch. 8.
C. Thomas, 'The character and origins of Roman Dumnonia', in
Rural Settlement in Roman Britain, 1966, p. 64.
C. E. Stevens, 'A lady of quality from Roman Devonshire', *Trans.
Devonshire Assn.* 84 (1952) p. 172.

Sites to Visit

The City Walls Best seen in Post Office Street and Southernhay West, in Northernhay Gardens and from South Street to the river.

The South Gate The tower is marked out on the west side of South Street, near the Inner By-pass.

The Baths Nothing visible.

Rougemont House Museum, Castle Street All finds from excavations in the city are housed here. Attention is drawn to the mosaic from Catherine Street, the glass vessels from the British Home Stores site, and to the decorated Samian pottery.

The new excavations by John Collis and Michael Griffiths, are being carried out in the car park between Waterbeer Street and Paul Street, and at the site of St Mary Major church opposite the west front of the Cathedral. All profits from the sale of this booklet will be given to the excavation fund. Readers and visitors are invited to make their contribution either on the site or in the Museum.

Acknowledgements

The author is indebted to the Devon Archaeological Society for the loan of blocks for Plates I, V and VI, and for permission to reproduce Fig. 4 and Plates II and VII, all previously published in the Society's Proceedings. Fig. 3 and Plate VIII are reproduced from *Roman Exeter*, 1952, History of Exeter Research Group monographs No. 8.

www.ingramcontent.com/pod-product-compliance
Lightning Source LLC
Chambersburg PA
CBHW031448280326
41927CB00037B/400